THE LIVING
RAIN
FOREST

NIC BISHOP

Learning Media

CONTENTS

1 THE RAIN FORESTS OF THE WORLD

Tropical rain forests grow in places where it is **humid** all year and rains a lot. This is a perfect environment for many plants and animals. Rain forests cover only a small part of Earth's surface but are home to an amazing variety of life.

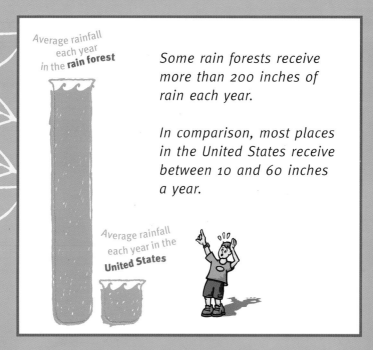

Average rainfall each year in the **rain forest**

Some rain forests receive more than 200 inches of rain each year.

In comparison, most places in the United States receive between 10 and 60 inches a year.

Average rainfall each year in the **United States**

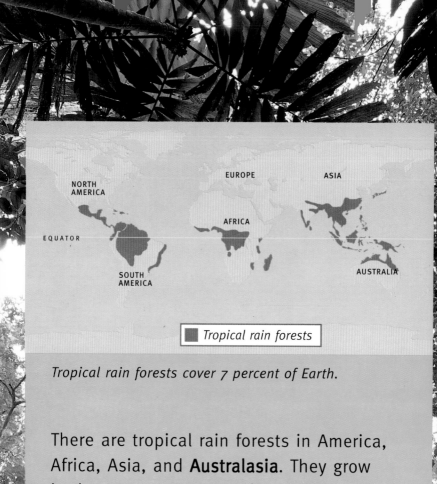

NORTH AMERICA

EUROPE

ASIA

AFRICA

EQUATOR

SOUTH AMERICA

AUSTRALIA

■ *Tropical rain forests*

Tropical rain forests cover 7 percent of Earth.

There are tropical rain forests in America, Africa, Asia, and **Australasia**. They grow in the warm areas near the **equator**. The largest area of rain forest is in the basin of the Amazon River in South America. It spreads from the Andes mountains to the Atlantic Ocean, 1,500 miles away.

2 THE MULTILAYERED RAIN FOREST

Inside the rain forest, plants and animals are everywhere. At first glance, it looks like a jumbled mess, but there are actually four layers of growth in the forest. Each layer has its own **population** of plants and animals.

The Emergent Layer
90–150 feet

The Canopy
60–90 feet

The Understory
30–60 feet

The Forest Floor
0–30 feet

THE FOREST FLOOR

At the bottom is the forest floor. This layer is shaded and sheltered by the trees above. The ground is covered with damp, rotting **vegetation**. Only a few plants, such as ferns and mosses, grow here because there is so little light.

*Animals that live on the forest floor, such as this tapir, are very quiet and shy. They are always on the lookout for **predators**, such as jaguars and human hunters.*

THE UNDERSTORY

Next comes the middle layer, the understory. Here bushes and small trees grow slowly in the shade of the giant trees above. Most of the understory trees spend all their lives in the shade, but a few eventually struggle up into the layer above.

THE CANOPY

The canopy is where the treetops finally reach the sunlight. The foliage, or leaves, of most trees is in this layer. It forms a dense roof that looks almost solid from above. When it rains, it can take up to ten minutes for the water dripping through the leaves to reach the forest floor.

THE EMERGENT LAYER

Only a few very tall trees break through the canopy into the emergent layer. Their branches sway freely in the breeze and enjoy the sunlight. During a big storm, an old emergent tree may be blown over. This opens a big hole in the canopy that smaller trees are able to grow through.

3 THE SUNLIT CANOPY

The canopy is the busiest part of the rain forest. The leaves, flowers, and fruit that grow there provide food for monkeys, birds, insects, and other animals. There are twice as many **species** living in the canopy as on the forest floor.

Canopy animals use climbing plants and long branches as pathways to get from tree to tree. They can follow these treetop trails for days and never have to visit the forest floor. Many animals are also very good at leaping between branches. The saki of South America is often called the flying monkey because it can easily jump a 30-foot gap.

Capuchin monkeys travel in noisy groups. They feed in the canopy but also swoop down to the lower levels to hunt small animals and insects, using their tails for balance and to hold branches.

VINES

Vines such as lianas grow up to the canopy by climbing on other plants. That way, they can reach the sunlight without having to grow a sturdy, thick trunk. Some vines use their roots to cling onto trees; others have sharp hooks or **tendrils**.

Liana vines wind their stems around the trunks and branches of trees. As a vine grows from branch to branch, it can tangle several trees together, as if they were tied with thick ropes. A liana can be more than 300 feet long by the time it reaches the canopy.

Some plants, such as the bromeliad, take root on the branches of canopy trees. Bromeliads catch rain and hold it in small pools between their leaves. Small creatures, such as frogs, salamanders, insects, and even crabs, live in these pools.

4 THE CREATURES OF THE RAIN FOREST

Scientists have found over one and a half million different species of living things on Earth. But there are many more yet to be discovered, especially in the rain forest. Nobody knows exactly how many species there may be. Scientists think that there could be up to ten million – maybe more!

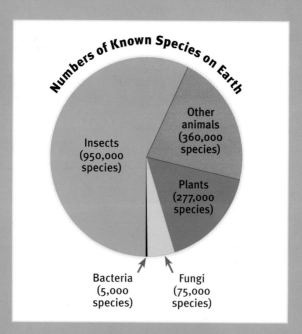

Numbers of Known Species on Earth

Other animals (360,000 species)

Insects (950,000 species)

Plants (277,000 species)

Bacteria (5,000 species)

Fungi (75,000 species)

INSECTS

A huge number of insects live in the rain forest, including ants, termites, bees, flies, wasps, mosquitoes, butterflies, beetles, and grasshoppers. Many of these live on the forest floor.

*Every day, thousands of leaf-cutter worker ants climb up into the canopy. They snip pieces of leaves with their sharp jaws and carry them back to their underground nest. The ants then eat the **fungus** that grows on the leaves. A large leaf-cutter nest may contain as many as five million ants. The trail of worker ants marching across the forest floor and up into the canopy can stretch for hundreds of feet.*

The hairs on this caterpillar form a barrier that prevents small wasps and ants attacking it.

The fallen leaves and rotting wood are the perfect home for insects. Many insects feed on the leaves, wood, fruit, and flowers that fall to the forest floor. Without the insects that feed on this material, the rain forest would soon be buried in its own rotting vegetation.

Tarantulas aren't insects — but they eat them. Sometimes they eat small birds and frogs too!

Some plants protect their leaves with poison, but many insects, like this grasshopper, have **adapted** to feed on these plants. This means that they can eat the poisonous leaves and not be harmed.

Rain forest butterflies often have long wings, which are perfect for gliding in the calm air beneath the canopy. This is a zebra longwing.

FROGS

The rain forest is a perfect **habitat** for frogs. They need to live in a damp environment because their skin is not waterproof. If a frog's skin dries out, it can die.

This is the red-eyed tree frog. Rain forest frogs also live in burrows or between the leaves of plants.

More kinds of frogs are found in rain forests than anywhere else in the world.

The amazing glass frog of South America has a body that you can see through. You can even watch its tiny heart beating!

The flying frogs of Asia have large paddle feet. They hold them out in the air to help them to glide from one tree to the next.

Tree frogs have suckers on the tips of their toes so that they can climb on slippery leaves. They can even hang upside down by their toes.

This leaf toad lives on the forest floor, where it feeds on small insects.

SNAKES

Most snakes in the rain forest are small and feed on birds, mice, and frogs. The biggest rain forest snake is the anaconda of South America. It can grow to be 36 feet long, and it can eat small deer.

This snake has large eyes to help it see in the dark. It searches the understory for frogs to eat.

This boa has just had a huge meal and will not need to eat again for several weeks. Snakes can separate the bones in their jaw. This allows them to swallow very large prey.

Snakes like to hunt at night. They have special ways of finding their **prey** in the darkness.

Snakes don't have ears, but they can feel the vibrations that other animals make as they crawl along the ground.

Whenever a snake flicks its tongue, it is tasting the air to see if it can find (taste) the smell of its prey. If its forked tongue picks up a scent, the snake knows which way to head for dinner.

MONKEYS

Monkeys like to travel in groups and stop in trees where there is lots of fruit and leaves to eat. Monkeys don't often climb down to the forest floor. They sleep among the branches of the trees.

Monkeys are the acrobats of the forest. They use their tails to keep their balance and to hold onto branches.

Spider monkeys use their long arms, legs, and tail to swing through the canopy faster than a person can run. They can even pick fruit with their tails!

Monkeys keep in contact by calling to each other across the treetops. One of the loudest is the howler monkey, which can be heard 2 miles away.

BIRDS

Birds play an important role in the rain forest. Some help plants to survive by carrying pollen from flower to flower. Others spread plants' seeds in their droppings.

The smallest bird in the rain forest is the hummingbird. Some hummingbirds are not much bigger than bumblebees.

The largest rain forest bird is the cassowary of Australasia. It is almost as tall as a person. It cannot fly and lives on the forest floor.

The toucan has the largest beak of any bird in the rain forest. It eats fruit and sometimes lizards and other small animals.

Perhaps the prettiest and noisiest birds of the rain forest are the parrots. They have large, powerful beaks that they use to crack open nuts. Their feet are also very good at holding things. Macaw parrots, like this one, often fly in groups. They zoom through the canopy like a feather rainbow.

5 SURVIVAL IN THE RAIN FOREST

HIDE AND SEEK

There are insects everywhere in the rain forest, but sometimes it's hard to see them. To hide from predators, many use **camouflage**. They have bodies that look like leaves, lichens, or twigs.

Many of the hunters of the rain forest, like the jaguar and ocelet, also use camouflage. Their spotted brown, yellow, and black coats match the patterns of light and shade on the forest floor. This helps them creep up on their prey unnoticed.

This katydid looks like a leaf – it even has small holes to look as if insects have nibbled it.

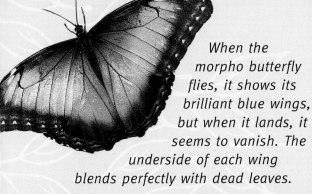

When the morpho butterfly flies, it shows its brilliant blue wings, but when it lands, it seems to vanish. The underside of each wing blends perfectly with dead leaves.

The green chameleon is suited to life in the canopy. It moves very slowly and is hard to see among the foliage.

PRETTY AND POISONOUS

Other animals and insects in the rain forest protect themselves from predators by using poison or stinging hairs. They are brightly colored so that their enemies will recognize them and leave them alone. In the rain forest, there are many poisonous butterflies, caterpillars, grasshoppers, stick insects, and bugs.

These caterpillars have hairs that sting if you touch them.

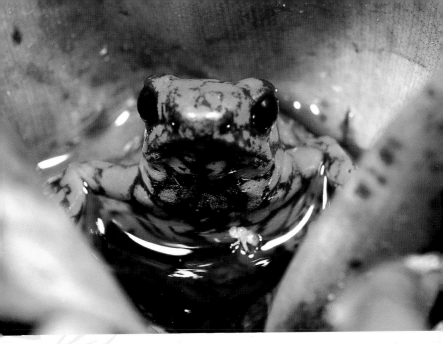

The dart frog is one of the most poisonous creatures in the rain forest. It is so **toxic** that you cannot pick one up. It is called the dart frog because people living in the rain forest use the poison from the frog's skin on their blow darts. They use these darts to hunt birds and small animals for food.

6 RAIN FORESTS AND PEOPLE

Scientists are always discovering new plants in the rain forest. They hope that some may contain chemicals that can be used to make new medicines. Many of the medicines that we already use come from rain forest plants.

This scientist has climbed up a rope to collect canopy plants. It is dangerous and difficult work.

While some people come to the rain forests to study them, there are others who have always lived there. They are the **indigenous** people of the rain forest, and they have adapted to life there. They are skilled hunters and know many things about jungle plants.

Rain forests are a precious **resource**. As well as drugs for medicine, many other useful things come from the rain forest. The cocoa in chocolate comes from a rain forest plant as well as coffee, bananas, and rubber.

But rain forests are in danger. They are being cut down for timber and to clear space for cattle, crops, and mining. Huge areas of rain forest are destroyed every day. This causes serious problems. Plants and animals in the rain forest depend on one another. Life there is very fragile. As more rain forests are destroyed, many of these plants and animals are lost forever. This affects everyone – not only the people who call the rain forest home.

GLOSSARY

(These words are printed in bold type the first time they appear in the book.)

adapted: adjusted to live in different or new conditions

Australasia: Australia, New Zealand, and the islands of the southwest Pacific

camouflage: the color of an animal that allows it to hide

equator: an imaginary line that goes around the middle of Earth

fungus: plant-like growths, such as toadstools, mushrooms, and molds

habitat: the natural home of a plant or animal

humid: warm and moist

indigenous: belonging to a particular country or area

population: all the inhabitants of a place

predator: an animal that hunts other animals for food

prey: an animal that is hunted by another animal for food

resource: something that provides useful things

species: a group of animals or plants that is different from all other groups

tendrils: a thread from a climbing plant that helps it to hang onto other plants

toxic: poisonous

vegetation: plants

INDEX